Great Scientific
Questions and the
Scientists Who
Answered Them™

HOW DO WE KNOW

THE NATURE OF

THE OCEAN

NATALIE GOLDSTEIN

Great Scientific
Questions and the
Scientists Who
Answered Them™

HOW DO WE KNOW
THE NATURE OF
THE OCEAN

THE ROSEN PUBLISHING GROUP, INC.
NEW YORK

For all the fish in the sea

Published in 2005 by The Rosen Publishing Group, Inc.
29 East 21st Street, New York, NY 10010

Copyright © 2005 by The Rosen Publishing Group, Inc.

First Edition

Library of Congress Cataloging-in-Publication Data

Goldstein, Natalie.
How do we know the nature of the ocean/by Natalie Goldstein.—1st ed.
    p. cm.—(Great scientific questions and the scientists who
    answered them)
Summary: Examines mankind's discoveries of the nature of the Earth's seas, how they were formed, and their role in regulating climate and weather. Includes bibliographical references and index.
ISBN 1-4042-0079-7 (library binding)
1. Ocean—Juvenile literature. 2. Oceanography—Juvenile literature.
[1. Ocean. 2. Oceanography.]
I. Title. II. Series.
GC21.5.G65 2004
551.46—dc22

                                               2003021815

Manufactured in the United States of America

Cover: Ocean waves crash against the shore of Nantucket, Massachusetts.
Cover inset: A satellite image of the earth.

Contents

1

Early Explorers of the Ocean

Carefully lettered in Latin on early European maps, in the regions beyond the known world, was the expression "Here live monsters." This was the medieval European notion of what lay within the vast and unknown waters that stretched to the ends of what many then believed was a flat earth. But in spite of fears of swarms of terrifying sea monsters

and the unthinkable prospect of falling off the edge of the earth, the quest for quicker trade routes compelled many Europeans to throw caution to the wind and take to the high seas. Our understanding of the ocean began with these fearless explorers. But they were not the first to link their fate with the sea.

Between 20,000 and 50,000 years ago, the islands of Australia and New Guinea were settled, most likely by people who set out by boat from Southeast Asia. The Lapita culture arose in New Guinea around 1600 BC, and these people later colonized Tonga and Samoa and became known as Polynesians. The Polynesians are recognized as the world's first great seafarers.

At least 3,000 years ago, the people of Polynesia expanded their settlements throughout the tropical Pacific. In wooden canoes crafted with tools of stone and coral, the Polynesians sought out islands suitable for settlement. They had no set destination—just a belief that they would find habitable islands. Without a compass or chart, they navigated by the stars at night and observed the flight of seabirds by day. They understood the behavior of the sea, noting the patterns of waves and swells that indicated a recent encounter with an island, and marking the reflections of clouds on the water and the bits of debris that floated on the waves. Obviously the sea was no lair of monsters for the Polynesians. They were such skilled and fearless seafarers that by 300 BC they had settled Tahiti and the Cook Islands. By AD 300 they had reached Easter Island. A century later they settled Hawaii, which is 2,000 miles (3,219 kilometers) from any island.

After the Polynesians, the world's greatest seafarers were the Vikings of Scandinavia, who ruled the northern seas between AD 800 and 1050. The Vikings perfected their ships' design after thousands of years of trial and error on the unforgiving North Sea. By the Middle Ages, the Vikings had fleets of thousands of longships—long, lean wooden boats capable of traveling great distances over the open ocean at remarkable speed. The dragon-prowed ships were not only fast and seaworthy, they were highly maneuverable, even in shallow coastal waters. The Vikings were the terror of Europe, invading

and conquering parts of Britain, Ireland, and continental Europe. They invaded and settled Iceland. When he was banished from Iceland for committing murder, Erik the Red sailed west, discovering Greenland. Leif Eriksson, Erik's son, inherited his father's adventurous spirit. When his vessel blew off course, he and his crew settled for a time in Newfoundland, Canada. They were the first Europeans to set foot in North America, 500 years before Columbus.

THE AGE OF EXPLORATION

In 1275, Marco Polo began his long land and sea voyage from Europe to Asia, spending a good deal of time in China and returning to Venice in 1295. Polo's travels whetted the European appetite for spices, silks, and other "exotic" Asian goods. In the 1400s, the Turks controlled the overland routes between Europe and the Middle East and Asia. European merchants, hoping to circumvent Turkish power, funded expeditions

Marco Polo spent seventeen years in the court of Kublai Khan before returning to Venice. The voyage home lasted two years and took the lives of 600 passengers and crewmen.

to find a direct ocean route to eastern Asia. A new type of ship, called a caravel, had both square and triangular sails, which made long ocean voyages possible. By the mid-1400s, the Portuguese had roughly mapped much of the west coast of Africa. In 1487, Bartolomeu Dias's ship was caught in a violent storm off the coast of southwestern Africa. To save his ship, Dias headed east into the Indian Ocean. Dias was the first European to sail around the southern tip of Africa—the Cape of Good Hope—and open a sea route to India and the Far East.

In 1492, Christopher Columbus set sail from Spain, hoping to find a route to Asia by sailing west across the Atlantic Ocean. On October 12, Columbus landed on the island of Hispaniola (San Salvador) in the New World. In 1513, Vasco Núñez de Balboa sailed across the Atlantic to what today is Panama. He was the first European to see the eastern shore of the Pacific Ocean. Balboa proved that the New World was a landmass situated between Europe and Asia.

Ferdinand Magellan left Spain in 1519 and sailed across the Atlantic to Brazil, then around the tip of South America and into the Pacific. In 1521, after three months crossing the Pacific Ocean, the starving sailors made landfall on Guam to gather lifesaving supplies. Though Magellan was killed in a battle in the Philippines, expedition survivors crossed the Indian Ocean, sailed around the Cape of Good Hope, and reached home in 1522, having successfully completed the first voyage around the world.

The earliest sailors navigated by taking sightings of the sun or establishing a ship's position in relation to

Much of what we know about the voyage of Ferdinand Magellan comes from the diary of one of his Italian crew members. For instance, it took Magellan's fleet thirty-eight days to pass through the Strait of All Saints, later renamed for him.

the North Star. The farther north a ship is, the higher in the sky the North Star appears to be, or the lower the sun appears to be. This was a crude and imprecise means of determining a ship's latitude (its distance north or south of the equator). Sailors used an astrolabe, a sighting stick with a wooden or brass disk with degrees measured along the edge, to estimate latitude.

By the fifteenth century, European sailors were familiar with the compass, which had been invented in China centuries before. The earliest compass was a simple piece of wood with a magnetized needle floating

In the eighteenth century "Britannia ruled the waves," but its ship captains still had no way to determine their longitude, their position east or west of some standard line, or meridian. In 1714, the British government offered a monetary prize to the inventor of an instrument that could determine longitude. The award went unclaimed for twenty-three years. In 1728, carpenter and clock-maker John Harrison began tackling the longitude problem. He realized that what was needed was a chronometer, an accurate timepiece that could withstand the motion of the sea and provide precise readings of shipboard time. Longitude can be calculated by a "sea clock" because the earth rotates 360° in twenty-four hours, or 1° every four minutes. By comparing the time on a chronometer with the known time at a standard point on the planet, sailors can calculate their longitude.

Harrison built his first chronometer in 1735, but it was too unwieldy for use on a ship. He kept improving his design, and in 1762, he produced a compact, lightweight, and extremely accurate chronometer. Greenwich, England, was established as the prime meridian, or 0° longitude, the site from which all longitude is calculated. Though Harrison's invention worked, it was not until 1773 that he received all the prize money.

in a dish of water. The needle rotated until it pointed toward magnetic north. At this time, too, sea captains determined their position by dead reckoning, a calculation involving estimates of a ship's speed (determined by throwing a log overboard with a knotted rope and timing how many knots in the reel unwound during one minute of sailing, using a minute glass). Combining the estimated speed with the compass direction gave some indication, however hazy, of a ship's progress.

Little was known about ocean currents, even into the eighteenth century. Currents were mapped by calculating "drift." Drift was the difference between the

expected location of a ship, based on the direction it was supposed to be going, and its actual location, which more often than not diverged considerably from expectations. The degree of drift was attributed to surface currents. Crude maps of these currents were used by early European seafarers.

CAPTAIN COOK

James Cook (1728–1779) was one of the founders of modern oceanography. Cook was born in Marton, England. His father was a farm laborer; Cook also worked as a farm laborer and grocer's assistant before his career on the sea began. Captain Cook took his first command at sea in 1766, on board the British ship *Endeavour*. During his first voyage, Cook sailed throughout the southern Pacific Ocean, charting previously unknown territories. He was the first European to set foot in New Zealand and Australia. He named Botany Bay for the wondrous plants he found there. He

Captain James Cook sailed into Botany Bay on April 29, 1770, and shortly thereafter proclaimed New South Wales, Australia, as a British possession. The name Botany Bay is inspired by all the variations of flora Cook's crew found in this new territory.

mapped the Great Barrier Reef and numerous Pacific islands. He continued finding and mapping far-flung South Pacific islands during his second voyage (1772–1775) and even sailed into the Southern Ocean on an approach to Antarctica.

Captain Cook is renowned for the meticulous maps he drew and for his keen observations of the

ocean and the plants and animals of the islands he visited. He was a master navigator and sailor, a superb cartographer, a great writer, and a decent artist. He was also one of the first captains to carry foods rich in vitamin C on his expeditions to prevent the dreaded scourge of sailors—scurvy.

In 1776, the restless Cook took to the sea again, this time seeking, and failing to find, the legendary Northwest Passage from the Pacific to the Atlantic. He stopped at the Sandwich Islands (Hawaii) for a time, and then sailed up the coast of North America, mapping, observing, and recording as he sailed as far as he could go into the Bering Strait. On returning to Hawaii for the winter, Cook was killed by the native people. Cook's contributions to science rest on his detailed and voluminous writings and drawings. His careful observations were key in launching the scientific study of the seas.

2
Global Waters

Most people have likely experienced the saltiness of seawater. Most people are also aware that river and lake water is fresh, not salty. For centuries, people wondered from where the sea's salt came. In the mid-eighteenth century, the renowned Scottish geologist James Hutton recognized that the salt in the sea comes from the wearing away of rocks on

land. Erosion of rock by freshwater carries enormous quantities of minerals, including salts, into the oceans. Each year, about 2.75 billion tons of dissolved substances wash off the land and into the sea. Erupting volcanoes also contribute minerals to the oceans.

Advances in chemistry during the seventeenth and eighteenth centuries enabled scientists to analyze the mineral content of seawater and determine the elements and compounds that constitute it. In 1674, the chemist Robert Boyle (1627–1691) determined the salinity of ocean water by measuring how much chloride it contained (table salt is sodium chloride, NaCl). The average salinity, or degree of saltiness, of the ocean is approximately 3.5 percent. This may not seem like much, but it means that one cubic mile (4 cubic kilometers) of seawater holds 166 million tons of salt! Ocean salinity varies depending on several factors, including the rate of evaporation, the amount of precipitation, the flow of freshwater from rivers, and the amount of sea ice, if present. Thus, the Red Sea, which is in a hot, dry climate (high

Robert Boyle is credited for separating modern chemistry from the practice of medieval alchemy. He was a founder of the Royal Society.

evaporation, low precipitation) is very saline, about 4 percent, while the Bering Sea in the North Pacific is in a cold (little evaporation), wet region, so its salinity is closer to 3.2 percent.

Some of the minerals that enter the ocean are taken up and used by marine plants and animals. The bicarbonate that forms when rain erodes limestone is used by sea creatures to make their shells. Other minerals are taken up as nutrients. Oxygen enters the ocean mainly through wave action at the surface. Marine animals breathe the oxygen dissolved in seawater. The ocean's surface absorbs carbon dioxide gas from the

atmosphere. Tiny marine plants, called phytoplankton, take in this carbon dioxide during photosynthesis. The amount of dissolved salts in ocean water determines one of its most important properties—its density. Cold, saline water is denser than warmer, fresher water. Seawater's density has a huge impact on ocean circulation and thus on the global climate.

OCEAN CIRCULATION

On one of his trips to London before the American Revolution, Benjamin Franklin (1706–1790) was asked if he knew why it took two weeks longer for mail to travel by ship from England to Rhode Island than for the return journey. The puzzled Franklin asked his cousin Tim Folger, a whaler, if he knew why there was such a huge time difference in traveling the same route in different directions. Folger responded immediately. Colonial whalers were familiar with a "gulf stream," a powerful current that increased the speed of ships moving east with it. Obviously, the British were unfamiliar with this current and unaware that they were sailing against it on the trip west. Franklin asked his cousin to sketch the Gulf Stream, and it was added to the maritime charts of the Atlantic.

One hundred years later, the Gulf Stream was scientifically studied and mapped. As it turned out, it was Franklin's great-grandson, Alexander Dallas Bache, then superintendent of the U.S. Coast Survey, who initiated further study of this powerful current. It was Bache's good luck to have on his staff Lieutenant Matthew Fontaine Maury (1806–1873), a self-trained scientist who was one of the founders of oceanography. Maury was born in Virginia and spent his youth in Tennessee. In the U.S. Navy, Maury became head of the Depot of Charts and Instruments, and he used his department's research ship to crisscross the current repeatedly. He also instructed sea captains to send him the pages of their logbooks pertaining to the current. In 1847, Maury published the first in his long series of Wind and Current

Charts, which became standard guides for ships crossing the Atlantic. Ships sailing east could hitch a ride on the Gulf Stream and reduce their voyages by thirty days or more. Ships heading west learned to avoid the strong current. Maury became known as the Pathfinder of the Seas. Maury used his fame for the Confederate cause when the Civil War broke out. He was sent to England as a spokesperson in an effort to acquire war vessels.

Some early studies of the Gulf Stream were rather whimsical but effective. In 1885, Prince Albert I of Monaco sailed the royal yacht to the Azores. He anchored there and proceeded to toss thousands of glass bottles and beer barrels into the Atlantic. Each contained only a message, written in ten languages, requesting the finder to please write to the prince to tell him where the bottle or barrel was found. From the hundreds of replies he got, the prince determined the path of the mighty Gulf Stream. He was the first to realize that the Gulf Stream, like many other currents discovered later, was in fact a huge, clockwise-flowing gyre, or circular current.

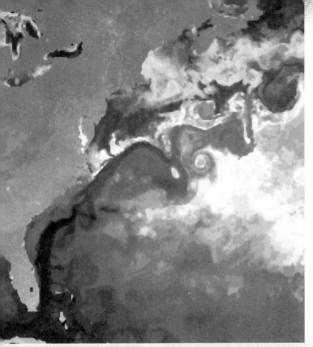

The Gulf Stream begins as a 50-mile-wide (80 km-wide) current. As it travels up the East Coast of the United States at 3 mph (4.8 km/h), it widens and cools considerably before separating into subcurrents.

Today we know that the North Atlantic gyre (of which the Gulf Stream is a part) is just one of many "wheels" that turn in the ocean, though it is one of the most powerful, carrying 2.4 billion cubic feet (70 million cubic meters) of water per second. There are gyres in all the world's oceans, but only five major ones: two in the Pacific, two in the Atlantic, and one in the Indian Ocean. In seas that span the equator, separate gyres occur in the northern and southern parts of those oceans. All gyres, except the Antarctic gyre, are constrained by the continents that rim them. The Southern Ocean current is not

hemmed in by land, so it flows unimpeded around Antarctica, effectively cutting the continent off from the rest of the world's warmer currents and keeping the continent frozen.

Surface gyres are driven largely by strong, steady winds, such as the east-to-west-blowing equatorial trade winds, which have been known to sailors for centuries. Winds flow from the poles toward the equator as a result of pressure differences caused by changes in temperature. However, they are then deflected by the Coriolis effect, named after Gustave-Gaspard Coriolis (1792–1843), the nineteenth-century French scientist who first described it. The Coriolis effect results from the rotation of the earth on its axis. In the Northern Hemisphere, winds moving south are deflected to the right, and in the Southern Hemisphere, winds are deflected to the left. The Coriolis effect has the same impact on ocean currents. Gyres in the Northern Hemisphere rotate clockwise; gyres in the Southern Hemisphere spin counterclockwise.

Winds and the Coriolis effect have their greatest influence on water at the sea surface. But what happens above affects everything below. Because of friction between layers of ocean water, a surface current sets in motion the layer of water just beneath it. The Coriolis effect acts on this submerged current, too, but twists it slightly differently, so it flows at a slight angle from the layer above. The second layer sets in motion an even lower layer, and so on, until each deeper layer of water is moving at an angle slightly different from the one above. The twisted spiral of water layers that results produces a pattern called Ekman drift, named after the Swedish oceanographer V. W. Ekman (1874–1954), who described it.

Ekman was a graduate student studying with the Norwegian explorer Fridtjof Nansen, who had made several expeditions to the Arctic during the 1890s. Nansen deliberately allowed his ship, the *Fram*, to become icebound, and then he recorded its drift. Over the course of a year, he noted that the vessel had not drifted with the wind, as he'd expected, but at an angle between 20° and 40° to the right of the wind. Nansen asked Ekman to figure out why this had happened. Ekman quickly formulated his drift theory and has been famous for it ever

As the Fram *slowly drifted in the ice, Fridtjof Nansen and a crew member took off on foot, reaching the highest latitude then attained.*

since. Ekman drift shows that an ocean gyre is like a huge wheel. The hub of the wheel is higher than the rim because of the angled, inwardly spiraling water layers beneath the surface. Because it's higher in the center, water flows downhill from the hub, and as it does, it too is twisted by the Coriolis effect.

The Gulf Stream and other gyres are part of the great, worldwide motion of the ocean known as the thermohaline circulation, the conveyor belt of currents that flows continuously through the seas. As its name suggests, the thermohaline circulation is driven by variations in the temperature and salinity of ocean waters. The thermohaline circulation was discovered by Benjamin Thompson (1753–1814), an American living in Germany (where he was dubbed Count Rumford), in 1797. The Massachusetts-born inventor and scientist was a Loyalist who left with the British in 1776. Thompson invented croutons, and it was per-haps while preparing hot soup that he was first inspired to make a scientific study of heat's effects on convection currents in the ocean. He described how the heat in ocean water "descends to where it will immediately begin to spread on the floor . . . and flow toward the equator." Thompson realized that the only place cold water could enter the oceans was at the poles and that this water warmed as it flowed toward the equator.

Thompson's theory went essentially untested until 1925, when the German ship *Meteor* crisscrossed

the Atlantic along thirteen lines of latitude between Cuba and the southern tip of South America. During two years at sea, the expedition's scientists made more than 9,000 measurements of ocean water temperature and salinity at 310 stations. The ship's data confirmed that, in the Atlantic, cold water becomes dense enough to sink all the way to the bottom at two key sites: the Weddell Sea off Antarctica and the North Atlantic off Greenland. The two sites are like cold-water spigots, pouring their icy liquid into the ocean. From each site, dense, ice-cold bottom waters flow toward the equator, warming, losing density, and rising as they go. At the equator, the two currents collide. The colder and denser current—the Antarctic current—attains a greater depth, thus deflecting the North Atlantic current upward and westward, forming the Gulf Stream.

In the early 1900s, most oceanographers believed that major ocean currents were relatively stable and unchanging. Research conducted by oceanographers

THE SARGASSO SEA

Near the hub of the North Atlantic gyre is a strangely still 2,000-square-mile (5,180 sq km) expanse of water called the Sargasso Sea. Because of its proximity to the gyre's hub, sea level on the Sargasso Sea is about 4 feet (1.2 m) higher than the rest of the Atlantic. The oval Sargasso Sea is an eerily placid region of light winds, weak currents, low precipitation, high evaporation, and exceptionally salty water. Lack of thermal mixing has made the Sargasso Sea a biological desert, without the plankton that form the base of nearly all ocean ecosystems. Yet the Sargasso Sea is not devoid of life. The sea is dominated by brown seaweed that is buoyed on the surface by air-filled, berry-size bladders. ("Sargasso" comes from the Portuguese word *sargaço*, which means "grape.") The seaweed, which floats freely along the surface, supports a unique community of organisms, including sargassum fish. Remarkably, each fall, eels migrate from Europe to an area of the Sargasso Sea near Bermuda to spawn and die. Eel hatchlings hitch a ride on the Gulf Stream for the three-year trip back to Europe.

Henry Stommel (1920–1992) and John Swallow (1923–1994) proved them wrong. These oceanographers began what is known as the mesoscale revolution, which showed that most of the ocean is in anything but a "steady state." Stommel and Swallow uncovered enormous variability in ocean currents, especially at a "midsize" (mesoscale) level. By 1973, leading MODE (Mid-Ocean Dynamics Experiment), Stommel revealed that ocean currents are constantly spawning midsize eddies, swirls of water up to 200 miles wide (322 km) that bud from the main current, persist for months or years, then fade back into the main stream. It has since been calculated that about 99 percent of the kinetic energy, or energy of motion, in ocean currents comes from variable mesoscale currents.

VERTICAL STRATIFICATION

Ocean water is highly stratified, or has many layers, and scientists have defined layers that differ markedly from each other. Each of these layers has dramatically different characteristics in terms of temperature, salinity, and density. The surface layer of the ocean, also called the mixed layer because winds cause extensive mixing of its waters, is relatively warm and extends to a depth of 300 to 1,500 feet (91 to 457 m). At the boundary of the mixed layer, there is a relatively abrupt and dramatic change in temperature, salinity, and density. This boundary is the thermocline, the dividing line between warm upper waters and cold deep water.

Determining the behavior of deep-water currents requires sophisticated equipment. The American oceanographer Henry Stommel was particularly interested in obtaining an instrument that could analyze deep-sea currents to test his hypothesis that cold countercurrents flowed beneath ocean gyres. The instrument envisioned by Stommel was designed and built by British oceanographer John Swallow. "Swallow floats" were introduced in the mid-1950s. Each float consists of a 10-foot-long (about 3 m) aluminum pipe supplied

John Crossley Swallow prepares to launch his swallow float. These floats gave the first direct and reliable data of deep ocean currents. Soon after, international programs began in oceanic research, such as the Mid-Ocean Dynamics Experiment (MODE).

with ballasts of varying densities. The ballast design was based on the principle that a float denser than the surface water would sink until it reached a depth at which the seawater was denser than it was. At this depth, the float would stop sinking and just float along with the current. By varying the density of the floats, Swallow could study any layer of the ocean.

Swallow floats were also outfitted with a transmitter whose pinging sound could be picked up by underwater receivers, which could track them as they were carried on a current.

Swallow first tested his floats in 1957, during a research expedition to Bermuda with Stommel. The oceanographers tracked the sounds of seven floats, charting currents at depths as great as 9,000 feet (2,743 m). Stommel's hypothesis was confirmed: floats nearer the surface traveled northward with the Gulf Stream; floats in deep water headed south with the countercurrent. Later research revealed that the ocean abyss actually has its own gyres, which churn in a direction counter to the surface gyre.

3

Plumbing the Depths

Before the late nineteenth century, people thought of the deep ocean as a flat, lifeless underwater plain—a bare wasteland beneath the world's seas. It was thought that deep ocean water was so dense and cold that nothing could live there. Many people even believed that at some great depth beneath the sea, the water was so dense that nothing could sink beneath it. People imagined shipwrecks floating eternally in this dense layer, never sinking, their sailors never finding rest.

To test his hypothesis that the deep ocean was lifeless, in early 1841 Edward Forbes (1815–1854), a failed artist and medical school dropout from Great Britain, dredged a site in the Aegean Sea. Forbes "confirmed" that below 300 fathoms (1 fathom equals 6 feet or 1.8 meters) nothing could survive. It was Forbes's bad luck that his dredge site is now known as one of the most lifeless sites in the world's seas. But even as Forbes came up empty-handed, expeditions to the polar seas by Sir John Ross dredged up animals such as starfish from seafloor depths of 4,800 feet (800 fathoms or 1,463 m) or more.

On December 7, 1872, the British ship *Challenger* left its port in England for a three-and-a-half-year ocean research expedition that would circle the globe. The *Challenger,* an old warship, had been stripped of its

Here, members are gathered on board Challenger. *The expedition, considered the birth of oceanography, was made with the cooperation of the British Admiralty, the Royal Society, and the British Treasury.*

guns and outfitted with laboratories stuffed with research equipment. The scientific expedition was led by naturalist Sir Charles Wyville Thomson (1830–1882), who, at the age of forty-two, felt he was too old for the job but went anyway.

Thomson's team charted about 140 square miles (636 sq m) of ocean floor, collected more than 4,000 new species of sea organisms, analyzed water samples from various depths, charted currents, and made depth soundings, that is, measured the depth to the bottom by lowering long lengths of lead-weighted ropes. At 362 stations, the exact depth of the sea was measured, water temperatures were determined, and bottom samples were dredged up. *Challenger*'s scientists disproved once and for all the concept of a lifeless seafloor. They also disproved the idea of a flat and featureless sea bottom. In its nearly 69,000-nautical-mile (79,404 mi or 127,788 km) journey, the *Challenger* had pretty well established the general contours of the ocean basins, which featured underwater mountains and deep trenches. The deepest spot the scientists found, off the Pacific's Mariana Islands, is today known as the Challenger Deep. It is the deepest site on earth, now measured about 36,000 feet (11,000 m) below the surface, more than 1 mile farther below sea level than Mt. Everest is above it.

SOUND WAVES

In 1912, the year the *Titanic* sank in the North Atlantic, the Canadian-born Reginald Fessenden (1866–1932), one-time assistant to Thomas Edison, began experimenting with echolocation, or measuring the distance of an object by its reflection of sound waves, as a way for ships to detect nearby icebergs. Fessenden knew that sound, not light, traveled well through water, and

he thought it was the key to locating underwater objects. The speed of sound underwater had been measured as nine-tenths of a mile per second, more than four times the speed of sound in air.

Using an electric contraption somewhat like an underwater doorbell, Fessenden sent sound waves through seawater and listened for their echoes. In the same way that tapping a hollow wall sounds different from tapping a solid wall, undersea echoes differ depending on the types of objects they encounter and bounce off. By analyzing subtle differences in the echoes, Fessenden could determine the types of objects—icebergs, shoals, or bottom sediment—that lay in the path of the emitted sound waves. Fessenden had discovered sonar. Fessenden was primarily interested in the military use of his new invention, and the U.S. Navy eagerly adopted sonar for detecting submarines. Sonar technology continued to be refined during the two world wars that followed its discovery, and it has been used on modern ships ever since.

Sonar became invaluable to scientists studying the seafloor. U.S. Navy physicist Harvey C. Hayes was the first to adapt Fessenden's discovery for use in deep-sea research. The Hayes Sonic Depth Finder allowed the operator to adjust the intervals at which sounds were beamed to the depths. This improvement overcame the tendency of earlier versions of the echo sounder to miscalculate the interval between the time a sound was emitted and the time its echo was heard, creating inaccuracies in distance measurements.

THE EARTH IN MOTION

In the sixteenth century, the Belgian cartographer Abraham Ortelius (1527–1598) hypothesized that, based on their shapes, it was likely that at one time all the continents had fit together, like pieces of a jigsaw puzzle. He thought that the Americas had been torn away from Europe and Africa and that this was evident on a map of the world. In 1858, French geographer Antonio Snider-Pellegrini (1802–1885) drew a map based on Ortelius's

idea. The map showed how snugly modern continents might, long ago, have fit together. At the time, Snider-Pellegrini's map was an interesting curiosity, but no one could imagine how continents could be ripped apart.

There the matter rested until the early twentieth century. In 1912, German meteorologist Alfred Wegener (1880–1930) revived the idea that more than 200 million years ago all modern continents had been part of a giant supercontinent, which he called Pangaea, and that some 100 million years later this landmass broke up, each continent drifting away from the others. Wegener supported his hypothesis, which he called continental drift, by noting similarities among fossils and rock formations throughout the world, as well as the remarkable fit of continental coastlines. Wegener also noted that coal beds in Antarctica were comprised of decayed and compressed tropical vegetation. Wegener concluded that at one time the frozen Antarctic had been near the equator and had drifted to its current position. Wegener's theory lacked one critical element. What force was strong enough to move entire continents across the planet?

Continental Drift

180 Million Years Ago

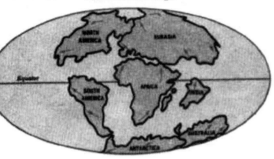

70 Million Years Ago

Present Time

Wegener proposed that the plates on which the continents sat simply plowed through the ocean floor. In subsequent years, British geophysicist Harold Jeffreys (1891–1989) proved this was impossible. Wegener's theory appeared to be dead.

In the 1950s, scientists at Columbia University's Lamont Geological Observatory in New York developed the Precision Depth Recorder (PDR), a device used to measure

Pangaea, Greek for "all land," separated into the subcontinents Laurasia and Gondwanaland. Today, NASA records this phenomenon using such technology as Global Positioning Systems.

seafloor depth with less than 1 percent error. Oceanographers Bruce Heezen, Marie Tharpe, and Maurice Ewing compiled and analyzed all the PDR records for the Atlantic Ocean to see what the PDR could reveal about seabed topography. The first hints of a submarine mountain range in the Atlantic were found by scientists aboard the *Challenger* in the 1870s. While taking soundings in the southern Atlantic, the scientists were perplexed by the shallowness of the water. They hypothesized that there might be a mountain down there, but they did not have the equipment to investigate further. (Many Europeans thought the *Challenger* had found the lost continent of Atlantis!) On one of its crossings of the Atlantic, the German ship *Meteor* had taken soundings that seemed to show a complete mountain range under the sea.

In 1959, the Lamont Geological Observatory scientists published the results of their detailed study of what was called the Mid-Atlantic Ridge. It had taken five years for Tharpe, then Heezen's graduate assistant, to fill in the details on their undersea map, which showed clearly the north-west line of the underwater mountain chain. The map revealed an ocean floor landscape of rugged mountains, crags, spires, and deep rifts.

In drawing her map, Tharpe noticed a V-shaped notch at the crest of the Mid-Atlantic Ridge. She pointed it out to Heezen because it looked to her like evidence of continental drift, a place where the ocean floor was pulling apart. Heezen compared Tharpe's V-shaped notches to the topography of the East African Rift, a site where the earth's crust was known to be spreading apart. They looked nearly identical. Then Heezen asked another graduate assistant to map the sub-Atlantic earthquake belt. When he compared this map with Tharpe's, he found that nearly all the quake epicenters were located inside Tharpe's V-shaped notches. Heezen became convinced that the Mid-Atlantic Ridge was geologically active. It was a place where the earth's crust was spreading apart, where the seafloor was cracking open. Turning to the extensive records kept on worldwide earthquake epicenters, Heezen noted that most of them occurred in a belt that wound around and through the

world's oceans. Though most of these ocean regions had not yet been mapped, Heezen concluded, correctly, that if Atlantic earthquakes occurred along submarine rifts, then all ocean earthquakes occurred along rifts. In their final 1959 report, the Lamont scientists showed that the Atlantic mountain range is not unique but is part of a string of mountain ranges that snakes through the oceans around the entire planet like the stitching on a baseball. The finding was revolutionary. Ocean ridges were key regions where continental drift was occurring. Wegener was vindicated.

Heezen and Ewing insisted that the mid-Atlantic rift was a widening volcanic fissure, a huge lava-filled crack in the earth's crust that was pushing the seafloor outward away from the rift in both directions. Continental drift was happening all the time where the seafloor was spreading and new crust emerged. But if new crust was emerging at rifts, what was happening to the old crust?

Between 1923 and 1938, Dutch geophysicist Felix Andries Vening Meinesz (1887–1966) logged more than

125,000 miles (201,168 km) crouched painfully inside small submarines as he studied the seafloor. In 1932, a young graduate student named Harry Hess (1906–1964) accompanied Vening Meinesz on a trip to the Puerto Rico trench, the deepest place in the Atlantic, 28,232 feet (8,605 m) below the surface. Vening Meinesz had determined that the force of gravity in the trench was abnormally low. He concluded that this anomaly occurred because in deep-ocean trenches, lightweight, low-gravity crust was being forced down into the earth, where it displaced dense, high-gravity material.

Hess was intrigued. He knew that the Mid-Atlantic Ridge rocks were volcanic and that heat was emitted from the rifts. He knew that low-gravity crust was disappearing into the seafloor at deep-ocean trenches. He also knew that deep-ocean dredging expeditions, hoping to find the oldest rocks on earth on the seabed, had instead come up with some of the world's youngest rocks. What did it all mean?

In 1960, Hess put it all together in a ground-breaking paper, later published as *History of Ocean*

Basins. Hess described his theory of seafloor spreading, suggesting that the earth's mantle, the layer just below the hard outer crust, is in constant motion. The crust, which appeared to be divided into about a dozen "plates," floated over the hot mantle beneath it. Molten mantle material is constantly emerging at mid-ocean rifts, building up the ridges as it cools and pushing older crust away from the ridge and across the ocean floor. When the older crust crashes into a continent, it is simply recycled as it is pushed down into the mantle at deep trenches near the continents. Hess described how instead of continents plowing through the oceanic crust they instead ride passively on mantle material that surfaces at the crest of the ridge and then moves laterally away from it.

Scientists had known for some time that as some minerals in molten rock cool, they become magnetized by the earth's magnetic field. When these rocks harden, their magnetic fields are permanently aligned with the prevailing magnetism. In the early twentieth century, British scientists Patrick Blackett

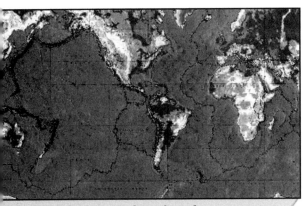

Volcanoes and earthquakes may occur at the boundaries of the earth's tectonic plates, illustrated here. Mountain ranges also rise at plate edges, as is the case with the Himalayas.

(1897–1974) and S. Keith Runcorn (1922–1995) found that basalts (igneous rocks) of different ages had magnetic fields that pointed in different directions, but not toward today's magnetic north pole. Some basalts, like those they found in Iceland, had magnetic fields that pointed south, not north. The scientists suggested that the earth's magnetic field had changed over time and that these shifts were manifested in the different magnetic fields of volcanic rock.

The idea that the earth's magnetic field could flip-flop over time intrigued Allan Cox (1926–1987), a graduate student of geology at the University of California at Berkeley in the early 1960s. He, Richard Doell, and Brent Dalrymple realized that they could prove that the earth's magnetic field wandered if they could show that all basalts of the same age had magnetic fields pointing in the same direction. To accomplish this, the students used a new technique for dating the age of rocks, based on the decay of radioactive potassium into argon. They began testing terrestrial volcanic rocks from California. Younger rocks had magnetic fields pointing north. Million-year-old rocks were oriented south. The scientists concluded that every million years or so the earth's magnetic field flipped. But then they started to find reversals in magnetism occurring every 100,000 years, then more and more irregularly. The researchers were forced to conclude that in the past 4 million years alone, the earth's magnetic field had reversed itself at least nine times.

Also in the early 1960s, aboard the HMS *Owen*, Cambridge University's Fred Vine and Drummond Matthews had been analyzing the peculiar "zebra stripes" on the seafloor of the Carlsberg Ridge in the Indian Ocean. Matthews and Vine were convinced that the seafloor stripes were visual evidence of the earth's magnetic reversals and proof of Hess's theory of seafloor spreading. Magma is extruded from the mantle all along the rifts in mid-ocean ridges. As the magma cools into rock, the rock becomes magnetized in the direction of the earth's magnetic field at the time the rock hardens. As new magma emerges, it pushes the older rock away from the ridge, then it too is magnetized as it hardens. Vine and Matthews realized that if seafloor spreading was really happening, the magnetic stripes on the seafloor should match the reversals of the earth's magnetic field over time. They did, and the ages of the rocks in each stripe confirmed Hess's theory. The youngest rocks, oriented toward today's magnetic north, were nearest the rift. The farther you went from the rift, the older the rocks were, and their magnetism correlated exactly with the magnetic reversals discovered by Cox and his team.

Vine and Matthews published their findings in 1963. However, few scientists gave it much credence. But Canadian geologist Tuzo Wilson was fascinated. He speculated that since lava emerging from a rift flows

equally to the east and west of the rift, the stripes on the seafloor should be magnetically symmetrical on either side of a mid-ocean ridge, and this symmetry should be maintained across the entire ocean basin. Further research proved Wilson right.

Hess and the other scientists were all proved right. Earth's magnetic field did flip. The seafloor was spreading, and the evidence for this spreading (magnetic striping) and the mechanism that kept it going (new crust emerging at rifts) were established beyond a doubt.

ON THE BOTTOM

The deep ocean has fascinated people as much as outer space, and aquanauts came long before astronauts. The first written reference to diving equipment comes from Aristotle, who described the wooden bell-shaped barrel, worn over the head, that was used during the conquest of Tyre by Alexander the Great in 332 BC. In 1716, English astronomer Edmund Halley constructed an enclosed wooden diving bell that was supplied with air through leather tubes extending to the surface. A diver could remain submerged in Halley's contraption for more than an hour at a depth of 60 feet (18 m).

Providing divers with air was only one of the problems facing inventors of diving equipment. The greatest challenge was protecting divers against the immense pressures of the deep. For every foot you descend in the ocean, the pressure increases by 0.442 pounds per square inch (psi). Thus at 200 feet (61 m), a common depth for divers, the pressure is about 100 psi. Atmospheric pressure on the surface of the earth is only about 15 psi. The body must be protected from these crushing pressures at moderate depths by inflating the diver's suit with air at the surrounding water pressure. In 1819, August Siebe invented a copper and leather diving suit that could be inflated, but it was cumbersome.

The next great achievement in underwater exploration was brought about by Jaques Cousteau (1910–1997), perhaps the most famous oceanographer of all time. Born in France, Cousteau had been fascinated with the ocean since childhood. He joined the French army as an officer in 1933, and then began his oceanic exploration. In 1943, he worked with French engineer Emile Gagnan to invent the Aqua-Lung. Their invention was

Jacques Cousteau's numerous documentaries and TV programs brought about public awareness to the need of protecting the earth's oceans and ecosystem.

lightweight and gave undersea explorers more freedom because there was no air hose tethering divers to the surface. Instead, a mouthpiece connected via a hose to a cylinder of high-pressure gas, which was worn on the diver's back. Cousteau was primarily interested in determining how long humans could live submerged beneath the sea in various types of exploratory vessels known as submersibles. Submersibles provide air and maintain normal surface atmospheric pressure within a reinforced structure. They have windows and equipment for analyzing and sampling the deep.

One of the first diving vessels, called a bathysphere, was invented by William Beebe and Otis Barton in 1930. The original bathysphere was a hollow steel sphere on the end of a cable. Its spherical shape distributed deep-ocean pressure evenly over its surface. In 1934, Beebe and Barton made their first record-breaking dive, descending to 3,028 feet (923 m). At this depth, the bathysphere was withstanding pressures of more than 1,360 psi. Their depth record stood for fifteen years.

As it turns out, the man who made the next technological breakthrough in submersibles was also the man who had pioneered development of stratospheric balloons. Auguste Piccard (1884–1962), a Swiss scientist and engineer, built his deep-sea bathyscaphe using the same principles he had applied to his balloons. Both have adjustable ballasts for controlling ascent and descent and a pressurized cabin for people to ride in.

Unlike Beebe's bathysphere, which was suspended on a cable, Piccard envisioned a free-floating submersible controlled by the weight of the ballast it carried. In 1948, Piccard became the first person to descend to the deep in an untethered submersible. His 6.5-foot-diameter (2-m-diameter) bathyscaphe was made of metal 3.5 inches (9 cm) thick to withstand undersea pressures. Its ballast was held to the craft magnetically and could be dropped quickly to permit a quick ascent. In 1953, with his son Jacques, Piccard descended in his most advanced submersible, the *Trieste*, to a depth of nearly 2 miles (3 km). Seven years later, Jacques and Don Walsh took the *Trieste* to the bottom of the Challenger Deep, 7 miles (11 km) beneath the ocean's surface.

In 1960, the submersible *Alvin* was developed at Woods Hole, Massachusetts, where it is still used to study the seafloor. *Alvin* can accommodate three people for undersea journeys of up to three days. The submersible has three thick viewing portholes, camera equipment, undersea lights, robotic arms capable of collecting seafloor samples, and a wide array of data-gathering equipment. In the early 1970s, *Alvin* was a key part of Project FAMOUS (French-American Mid-Ocean Undersea Study). It was during this expedition that the submersible descended into the inky unknown of the deep trenches at the center of mid-ocean ridges. The strangeness of what scientists saw there revolutionized our view of life itself. Two-and-a-half miles (4 km) beneath the surface of the Atlantic is a seascape so bizarre that it was beyond anything scientists had contemplated. They saw an endless expanse covered with black boulders and crags of broken stone and enormous twisted tubes of lava they dubbed "toothpaste lava."

In 1973, three scientists descended to the bottom of the Galápagos rift, near the islands Charles Darwin had made famous. They were hoping to determine why the centers of mid-ocean ridges, where red-hot magma rises, were unexpectedly cool. The scientists descended 7,500 feet [2,286 m] on board the *Alvin*. As they were

FROZEN CARBON BENEATH THE SEA

Buried beneath the floor of the deep ocean, at least 3,000 feet (914 m) below the seabed, lie deposits of methane, a compound of carbon. At these depths, pressures are so great and temperatures so cold that the methane, which usually occurs on the surface as a gas, is frozen solid. Because it is bound in a matrix of ice, the deposits are referred to as methane hydrates. This deep-sea methane is a waste product of bacterial digestion. Bacteria living in the deep-ocean sediment consume what little plant and animal debris floats their way and then excrete methane waste. The methane is deposited within a lattice of frozen water molecules, a process that allows a huge amount of methane to occupy a very small space.

Little is known about methane hydrates, but some energy companies are contemplating using these deposits as fuel. There are several drawbacks to this plan. First, methane is a greenhouse gas, so it would add considerably to global warming. Second, it would be both expensive and dangerous to extract the methane hydrates from beneath the ocean floor. Third, in the geological past, warming of deep-ocean currents caused these methane hydrates to melt and diffuse out of the ocean, causing catastrophic climate warming. Drilling for methane might generate enough heat to cause a chain reaction of melting methane hydrates, something no one wants to risk.

measuring water temperature and using the robotic arm to haul in a rock sample, they saw something that stunned them. The water above a nearby slope was shimmering, like the air above a sun-baked landscape. Boiling hot water shimmered upward out of a vent in the crust. Around it were giant mussels and clams, white crabs, enormous tube worms, and pink fish. The scientists had found a living oasis in the darkest depths of the ocean. New expeditions brought discoveries of new vents and new species of sea life—along with tube worms— were feathered worms, spaghetti worms, new species of shellfish, and sea anemones. What was it

about deep-sea vents that made them the focal point of entire ecosystems?

A deep-sea vent is a place where water sinks into a fissure and touches magma, becomes superheated, and shoots, shimmering and boiling, back up into the ocean through the vent, forming towering pillars, or chimneys, from minerals in the magma. Some geysers, called black smokers, are so laden with minerals that their water is black. As a rule, minerals are widely scattered in most of the deep ocean. But because they're so abundant at deep-ocean vents, the minerals have attracted and sustained vast colonies of bizarre animals that thrive only in this strange and unique environment. Deep-ocean vents are also teeming with thermophyllic (heat-loving) bacteria that thrive in the superheated waters.

Vent ecosystems are like no others on earth. No plants were found in the vent communities because plants need sunlight to survive. There is no sunlight at the bottom of the ocean. The animals that thrive around deep-sea vents do so by using the heat energy of the vent itself. Vent bacteria, at the base of the vent food chain, consume the sulfide in the hydrogen sulfide that spews from the vent. The bacteria use the abundant sulfur so efficiently that they multiply in the billions. In some white smoker vents, bacteria are so numerous that they pour out of the vents like smoke belching from a factory's smokestack. All vent animals depend on these bacteria for their survival. Some giant tube worms, for example, live in symbiosis, or close union, with bacteria and cannot survive without them. Some scientists speculate that life on earth began at deep-sea vents and was raised to the surface as mid-ocean ridges rose.

4

Oceans and Climate

t was not until the seventeenth century that the age of true scientific inquiry began, with the invention of instruments for measuring and analyzing the physical world. Previously, no one had been able to scientifically observe the weather and climate and how the oceans influenced them. In 1600, Galileo Galilei (1564–1642) invented the first thermometer. Galileo's friend, Evangelista Torricelli (1608–1647), moved to Florence, Italy, to work with him. Torricelli was conducting experiments with vacuums, and one day Galileo suggested that he use mercury in his tests. Torricelli took his advice, and in 1643, he made the first barometer. He filled a long glass tube with mercury and then inverted it and set it in a bowl. Some of the mercury flowed out of the tube, but a column of mercury about 30 inches (76 cm) high remained in the tube. Torricelli observed the behavior of the mercury in the tube over time, noting that its level sometimes rose and sometimes fell. After careful observation and analysis, Torricelli discovered that the variations in the height of the mercury in the tube were caused by changes in air pressure. When the air pressure was low, the mercury fell. When the air pressure was high, the level of mercury rose. Torricelli's barometer and the measurement of air pressure were critical to understanding how weather works.

Other meteorological discoveries and inventions followed. In 1667, Robert Hooke invented the

anemometer, a device for measuring wind speed. Robert Boyle showed that as a gas's volume is reduced, its pressure increases. Boyle's insights would lead to greater understanding of the behavior of air masses at different pressures. By 1792, John Dalton, an English chemist, was correlating barometric pressure with the heating and cooling of air. Dalton also analyzed the behavior of mixtures of gases. His findings were of great value to the new science of meteorology and enabled investigators to calculate the volume of water vapor in the air and to analyze cloud formation and precipitation.

Some of the most significant findings connecting the atmosphere to the ocean pertained to the trade winds, so named because they were so useful to transoceanic trade. This band of winds flows east to west along the equator. Edmund Halley, the discoverer of Halley's comet, wrote extensively about the trade winds. He correctly stated that the trade winds were generated by the intense sunlight hitting the equator. The heat causes the air masses to rise, pulling in cooler

This is a depiction of John Dalton collecting marsh fire gas for use in his experiments. His study of gases led him to formulate the atomic theory. By speculating that the main difference between atoms was mass, he created the table of atomic weights.

air from higher latitudes. Halley's ideas were expanded upon in 1735 by George Hadley, a London lawyer who much preferred climate research to arguing cases in court. Hadley showed that the east-to-west flow of the trade winds was caused by the rotation of the earth. Hadley also described what came to be known as Hadley cells, discrete north-south circular flows of air currents,

caused by temperature differences that occur at different latitudes. In 1835, Gustave-Gaspard Coriolis described how the rotation of the earth causes the curving deflection of these air currents to the east or west.

It was not long before scientists applied these findings about the air to the behavior of the ocean. Ocean currents are also deflected by the Coriolis effect. The heat and pressure of the air masses above affect the ocean surface, and the ocean affects the winds. For example, winds push water along the ocean surface, creating ocean currents, and the ocean adds water vapor to the atmosphere, which has a profound effect on weather. The trade winds were identified as the prime movers of equatorial ocean currents flowing east to west. As our understanding of the atmosphere increased, it became obvious that the atmosphere and the oceans were intimately connected. They were, in fact, two parts of a single system—the earth's climate—whose weather is nothing more than nature's attempt to even out the uneven distribution of heat on the surface of a rotating earth through circulation of the air and the sea.

EL NIÑO

There is one particular climate event that demonstrates how truly intertwined the oceans and the atmosphere really are. The term "El Niño" refers to a periodic warming of a tropical Pacific Ocean current. The effects of the warm current are usually noticed first in waters off the west coast of South America. Peruvian fishermen have known about this current for centuries, and because it occurs in December, around Christmas, they called it El Niño, Spanish for "the Christ child," or simply "the little boy."

El Niño is caused by disruptions of the normal atmosphere-ocean interaction in the equatorial Pacific. Normally, the trade winds blow along the equator from east to west. The west-moving winds push warm surface water west, away from South America and toward Indonesia. With the removal of warm surface water, conditions are ripe for upwelling of deeper, colder waters off the western coast of South America. Nutrient-rich cold water from the depths rises to the

surface, sustaining the Peruvian fisheries, which are vital to the survival of fish and fishermen. At the same time, the westward flow of warm surface water creates a huge warm water pool in the western Pacific.

During an El Niño, west-blowing trade winds slacken, stop, or begin to blow eastward. With weak or absent trade winds, warm surface water is no longer pushed westward. Because winds are no longer pushing warm water west, the upwelling of cold water off South America is dramatically reduced or stops altogether. During an El Niño, the trade winds are so weak that the warm water pool they normally create forms not in the far western Pacific, but in the central Pacific. This warm water pool actually flows eastward. Weather patterns are reversed. Rain clouds drench the central and eastern Pacific. Peru and other countries on the west coast of South America, which would normally be cool and dry, are drenched with rain. On the other hand, droughts afflict Indonesia, India, Australia, and other parts of Asia. El Niños intensify as they progress because less upwelling in the eastern Pacific further relaxes the trade

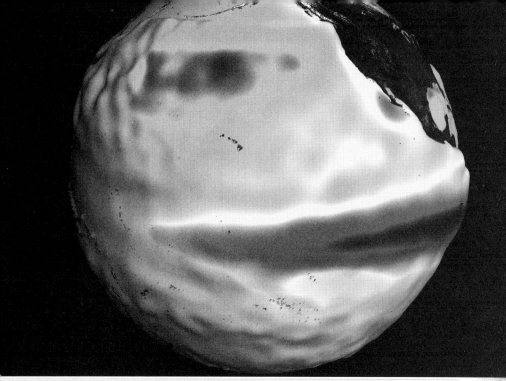

This visualization of the effect of El Niño depicts the anomaly that happens near the equatorial Pacific. The dark ridge indicates the warmer ocean temperature and the difference in height of the sea surface.

winds, which, in turn, move less water westward, which causes eastern waters to warm still more.

In 1877, the monsoon rains in southern Asia failed, and India experienced its worst famine in history. In 1904, the British sent Sir Gilbert Walker (1868–1958) to India to try to find out why the monsoons failed and, if it was possible, to find a way to predict future failures.

Walker studied decades of world weather records, particularly those describing air pressure over various parts of the ocean surface. Walker noted that surface pressures over the tropical Pacific varied in a pattern extending

Sir Gilbert Walker, criticized for connecting weather patterns over separate regions of the earth, was eventually proven right.

over many years. Most of the time, surface pressure in the eastern Pacific off South America is high, and the air is clear and dry. In contrast, air pressure over the warm water pool in the western Pacific is normally low, and rain is plentiful. Walker noticed that periodically the pressure difference, or pressure gradient, as it is called, between the eastern and western Pacific flattened out or even reversed itself. He called these periodic fluctuations the Southern Oscillation. He noted that changes in the Southern Oscillation correlated well with the failure of the Indian monsoons. He also showed that by carefully monitoring surface pressure in the Pacific, the intensity or absence of monsoon rains might be predicted.

Scientists began to monitor the Southern Oscillation continually from weather stations in Tahiti (the eastern Pacific) and Darwin, Australia (the western Pacific). Normally, surface pressure is relatively high in Tahiti and relatively low in Darwin. Scientists used data gathered at these two sites to develop the Southern Oscillation Index (SOI), which represents the relative strength of surface pressure in the eastern and western Pacific. A low SOI indicates a flattening of the pressure gradient and the onset of El Niño conditions.

In the 1950s, Norwegian American meteorologist Jacob Bjerknes (1897–1975) took Walker's work one step further. Bjerknes hypothesized that climate variations like El Niño were caused by large-scale disruptions in the

interaction between the atmosphere and the ocean. Bjerknes correlated Walker's Southern Oscillation with the onset of an El Niño event. He saw the connection between abnormally high sea surface temperatures, weak trade winds, and the heavy rains that accompany low SOI conditions in the tropical Pacific. Bjerknes gathered much of his data during the 1957 International Geophysical Year (IGY), which, as luck would have it, was a strong El Niño year. Because Bjerknes showed the close connection between El Niño and the Southern Oscillation, scientists now refer to this climate phenomenon as ENSO, the El Niño-Southern Oscillation.

But what causes El Niño? No one yet knows for certain. One theory involves the creation and movement of deep ocean waves, known as Kelvin waves, which flow hundreds of meters below the ocean surface. Normally, eastward-blowing winds in the tropical Pacific are very weak. When these winds become more powerful, they generate eastward-flowing Kelvin waves that depress the thermocline, the boundary between warm surface water and deeper cold water, throughout the tropical Pacific. Depressing the thermocline keeps cold water deeply submerged, so Kelvin waves increase sea surface temperature. When Kelvin waves reach the eastern Pacific, they generate Rossby waves, deep, slow-moving waves that propagate in the opposite direction, moving east to west, taking about nine months to cross the Pacific. Rossby waves may be responsible for terminating an El Niño event. As a Rossby wave crosses the Pacific, the thermocline begins to rise and sea surface temperatures cool.

OTHER OCEAN–ATMOSPHERE INTERACTIONS

The atmosphere responds fairly quickly to changes in incoming solar energy. The ocean, in contrast, responds slowly. The ocean is more like a heat-storage unit, whose energy-storing capacity is unimaginably huge. For example, the heat-storage capacity of the entire atmosphere is equal to the heat-storage capacity

of only the top 8.5 feet (2.6 m) of the ocean's surface. The upper regions of the ocean may take years or decades to respond to changes in the atmosphere. In the deep ocean, these changes may not be noticeable for millennia.

Ocean currents transport their stored heat around the planet. The Gulf Stream, for example, car- ries gargantuan amounts of heat to northwestern Europe, keeping it far warmer than its latitude should allow. The heat stored in the ocean also moderates the temperatures of nearby landmasses. Coastal regions of North America have more moderate weather—that is, fewer seasonal temperature extremes—than interior regions at the same latitude. Because of its heat-storing capacity, the ocean is warmer than the continents in winter. In the summer, it is cooler than the land. These temperature differences result in differences in surface pressure, which control regional wind patterns. In general, winds flow from areas where the surface is cold and the air pressure high toward areas where the surface is warm and the air pressure is lower. This creates seasonal circulation systems known as monsoons. The most famous monsoon occurs in India where, in summer, the subcontinent is baked by the sun and is far hotter than the ocean. Winds blow from the cooler Indian Ocean over the Indian subcontinent, dumping torrential monsoon rains on the land.

The atmospheric and oceanic circulation of heat energy also produces great storms known as hurricanes, or typhoons, as they are called in the Pacific. In 1821, William Redfield (1789–1857), a Connecticut shopkeeper, traveled across his hurricane-battered state to view the damage done by a storm. He noticed something odd. In central Connecticut, toppled trees had fallen toward the northwest. Trees torn down 50 miles (80 km) to the west had fallen toward the southeast. Redfield correctly speculated that this must have been caused by a circular whirlwind. A few years later, Redfield met Yale professor Denison Olmstead, and they began discussing the weather. Redfield described

what he'd seen after the hurricane, and Olmstead encouraged him to continue observing and recording the effects of hurricanes. For years after, Redfield gathered data about hurricanes. In 1831, he published his findings in a paper titled "Remarks on the Prevailing Storms of the Atlantic Coast of the North American States." His study confirmed the long-held hypothesis that hurricanes are rotating storms whose winds swirl counterclockwise around an eye, or calm center.

It was not until the early 1900s that advances in technology allowed meteorologists to collect enough accurate data to determine the nature of hurricanes. One of the most important tools turned out to be the telegraph, which was used extensively to transmit weather data. The father of Jacob Bjerknes, Norwegian meteorologist and physicist Vilhelm Bjerknes (1864–1951), was among the first to use the data to generate weather forecasts. During World War I, when Norway had no money for weather research, Bjerknes enlisted the help of Norwegian fishermen to supply

Hurricanes may occur up to fifty times worldwide each year. The width of a hurricane can range from 60 to 1,000 miles (97 to 1,609 km) wide. Here, Hurricane Isabel moves toward the North Carolina coastline in September 2003.

him with data. The information they passed on led to the formation of the polar front theory. The polar front theory describes how cold polar air masses blowing from east to west at high latitudes come into contact with warmer mid-latitude air masses moving west to east. The two fronts speed past each other and,

depending on other conditions, may generate all kinds of weather, including cyclonic storms, or hurricanes. Even slight variations in land and ocean temperature can cause a wavelike undulation in the colliding air masses. Sometimes these waves may dissipate, but if they occur over warm ocean water, there's a good chance that they'll intensify and form a hurricane.

Hurricanes form only over warm ocean water. The air above the ocean picks up tremendous amounts of water vapor from the surface. As the air rises and cools, the water vapor condenses, generating a huge amount of heat, which further destabilizes conditions in the low-pressure air mass. A hurricane forms when the winds near the ocean's surface begin to swirl inward and upward. The violently converging air mass continues to rise and forms thunderclouds. Rising air cools, and more water vapor condenses, which adds more heat to the air, which increases the intensity of the spiraling motion. Because of the Coriolis effect, hurricanes that form in the tropical Atlantic rotate and travel in a counterclockwise direction. The forward side of the storm carries the most destructive winds, which range from 74 miles per hour (120 kilometers per hour) in a category 1 hurricane to 156 miles per hour (250 km/h) or more in a category 5 storm.

GLOBAL WARMING

Life exists on earth because of the greenhouse effect—heat-trapping gases in our atmosphere keep the earth warmer than it would be without those gases. Among the most powerful greenhouse gases are carbon dioxide and water vapor. The ocean is an important sink, or storage reservoir, for carbon dioxide, which it absorbs from the air through the mixing action of waves at the surface. The carbon dioxide cycles through the oceans—for decades in surface waters, for millennia in the deep ocean. The atmosphere gets water vapor from the sea surface through evaporation.

There is by now nearly unanimous agreement among scientists that the burning of fossil fuels (coal, oil, gasoline) is adding unprecedented quantities of

carbon dioxide to the earth's atmosphere. Carbon dioxide emissions are warming the global climate at an unprecedented rate. For example, in the last 420,000 years, the highest concentration of carbon dioxide in the atmosphere was 300 parts per million (ppm), a concentration that occurred during the height of an interglacial tropical period. In 2003, the concentration of carbon dioxide in the air was more than 370 ppm. At this rate, the average global temperature might well increase between 9° to 15°F (5° to 8°C) over the next century or two. To put that in perspective, the average global temperature difference between the coldest part of an ice age and the hottest part of a tropical period is no more than about 9° to 11°F (5° to 6°C). In a natural climate cycle, this temperature increase occurs over a period of about 100,000 years, not centuries.

The burning of coal in generating stations such as the one pictured here contaminates local waters, as well as contributes to global warming. Global warming is happening at a faster pace now than in the last 10,000 years.

The world's oceans are showing the effects of climate change, with overall higher sea surface temperatures and rising sea levels. Warmer air over warmer surface water increases evaporation, so more water vapor enters the air. The more water vapor that enters the air, the greater the warming, which increases evaporation, which warms the climate still further, and so on. Increased water vapor in the air also leads to increased precipitation and more violent storms.

Though some scientists and policymakers had hoped that the oceans would absorb excess carbon dioxide from the atmosphere and promote global cooling, research seems to indicate otherwise. In 1999, scientists with NASA's Goddard Space Flight Center showed that warmer Antarctic waters caused significant declines in cold-water algae that take in lots of carbon dioxide. They've been replaced by species of algae that take in less atmospheric carbon dioxide. A 2001 study of the northern Pacific revealed that its absorption of carbon dioxide has fallen 10 percent in the past fifteen years.

Perhaps most worrying are the effects of global warming on ocean currents. In 1998, researchers with Princeton University's Geophysical Fluid Dynamics Lab (GFDL) reported that increased concentrations of carbon dioxide in the oceans will disrupt global ocean currents. Excess carbon dioxide cycles to the deep ocean, where it warms the water and causes thermal expansion. It also causes the melting of glaciers and increases precipitation due to higher air and ocean surface temperatures. Abnormally high precipitation interferes with ocean mixing. It causes the warm layer of surface water to inhibit the upwelling of cold, nutri-ent-rich water from the depths. This lid of warm water effectively blocks the absorption of carbon dioxide by the deep ocean. Scientists with the GFDL have shown that the faster carbon dioxide builds up in the air and in surface water, the greater the reduction in the ther-mohaline circulation in the world's seas. Researchers with the Rennell Center for Ocean Circulation detected a greater warming of Atlantic Ocean cur-rents, not near the surface as expected, but at depths

of 1.6 miles (2.6 km). The Atlantic's average depth is 2.2 miles (3.5 km). If carbon dioxide emissions double as expected, ocean surface temperature should increase between 3° and 7°F (2° to 4°C), with deep currents likely warming even more. Warming of such a magnitude may have catastrophic effects on the ocean-atmosphere system.

The North Atlantic gyre is powered by a region of cold, dense, salty water in the North Atlantic near Greenland. This "engine" maintains the North Atlantic Deep Water (NADW) circulation because its waters are 7 percent above normal salinity levels, creating a change in density. But there is evidence that more than 265,000 square miles (680,000 sq km) of the Greenland glacier is melting. Melting adds enormous quantities of fresh water to the NADW engine. Because both the air and the surface water in this region are abnormally warm, evaporation has increased, resulting in more freshwater precipitation over the NADW. All told, these huge inputs of fresh water are decreasing the salinity of the NADW at its source.

The NADW is the most vulnerable point of the climate system because this monumental deep-water circulation is dependent on a relatively small difference in salinity at its source. If its salinity is reduced, the NADW is weakened. If it's weakened too much, the NADW circulation may collapse completely. In the past, the weakening or collapse of the NADW initiated ice ages. The Gulf Stream carries huge amounts of heat to northwestern Europe. As the NADW weakens, the Gulf Stream also weakens and so carries less heat to Europe. Northern European winters and summers become colder. Soon, snow and ice remain on the ground all summer. More ice and snow accumulate the next winter, and the next summer the perpetually snow-covered region expands. In about a decade, an ice age begins over the Northern Hemisphere. Scientists have already noted a small but significant weakening of the NADW. As global warming continues, the NADW will likely weaken further.

The people of the South Pacific islands are desperately worried about global warming. Recently, the

11,000 residents of Tuvalu decided to evacuate their vanishing island home. In the last century, the sea level at Tuvalu has risen about 12 inches (30.5 centimeters), covering most of the island. Global warming causes sea levels to rise due to the melting of glaciers and polar ice and to thermal expansion. People on many other low-lying Pacific islands are preparing to see their homes disappear beneath the waves. In the United States, about half the population lives within 50 miles (80 km) of a coast. If global warming keeps raising sea levels, they too may be forced to relocate in the future.

The Origin and Fate of the Ocean

The oceans cover approximately 140 million square miles (364 million sq km) of the earth. They hold about 324 million cubic miles (1.4 billion cubic km) of water. Where did all that water come from? No one knows for sure, but there are a number of theories.

ORIGIN

Perhaps the oceans filled with water that was released through volcanic eruptions. The young earth was constantly shaken by erupting volcanoes. It's possible that these eruptions released water that had been bound inside rocks in the interior of the planet. Volcanoes emitted it as water vapor or steam, which then cooled into liquid and fell as rain. This is the "volcanic outgassing" theory of the origin of the seas.

Some scientists insist that there was never enough volcanic activity to release the amount of water needed to fill the oceans. They suggest that when the sun began to form from interstellar clouds, it began to rotate rapidly. Dust-laden gas was hurled away from the spinning star but was held in orbit around the sun's

Undersea volcanoes resemble their counterparts on land, such as the Paricutin volcano in Mexico, pictured here. Volcanoes exist in all of the earth's oceans, with 10,000 of them in the Pacific Ocean alone.

equator by the sun's gravitational field. The orbiting disk of dust contained bits of rock and ice. The orbiting dust and ice began to collide and fuse. These growing accumulations of rock and ice were the newly forming planets. The early earth's rocks therefore contained an abundance of water derived from ice.

The heat generated by the nearly constant collisions with asteroids, planetoids, and space rocks released earth's rock-bound water as steam. The steam hung in the ancient atmosphere, giving it a pressure 100 times what it is today. Japanese scientists studying this scenario believe that the ancient atmosphere contained an amount of water vapor equivalent to all the water in today's oceans. Eventually, the earth cooled and it started to rain. This rain would have had a temperature of about 600°F (316°C), the temperature at which water boils at 100 atmospheres of pressure. This collapse of the atmosphere lasted for millennia and emptied the atmosphere of most of its water vapor. The liquid filled the oceans. These first watery oceans would have been boiling hot. As the atmosphere rid itself of its vapory burden, its pressure decreased. Over time, lower atmospheric pressure reduced the temperature of the water filling up the oceans.

Because the oceans are so vast, people tend to think of them as limitless in every way. The oceans would always provide limitless amounts of fish and shellfish. They would afford a limitless expanse in which to dump limitless amounts of waste. Today we know that even the oceans have their limits, and in many ways these limits have been reached or exceeded.

OVERFISHING

In 1895, a Massachusetts fisherman hauled in a cod more than 6 feet long (1.8 m) and weighing 211 pounds (96 kilograms). At that time, the fabled abundance of cod off the coast of Massachusetts provided a good life for the fishermen who went out with fishing lines and nets in their small boats. By the turn of the century, technology provided improved means for catching fish. Trawl nets got larger. Sonar was used to locate schools of

Cod, pictured here in a 1932 fish market, is one type of fish now included on the list of endangered species. Most cod are caught between the age of two and four years—before having a chance to spawn.

fish. A good catch in 1890 was about 60,000 pounds (27,216 kg) per year. By 1920, fishermen harvested 120,000 pounds (54,5431 kg) per year. Then corporations entered the game. By the 1960s, factory ships were pulling in up to 1 million pounds (453,592 kg) or more of cod annually. Retail fish prices plummeted. To compete, small fishery operations invested in technology that made them equally efficient. By the 1970s, the North Atlantic cod fishery was near collapse. For the next two decades, fishery managers tried to calculate a safe and sustainable catch based on hazy projections of cod populations. Fishermen intensified their search for ever-dwindling stocks. By 1992, the cod were gone for good. Fisheries biologist Ransom Myers showed that there simply were not enough juvenile fish left to reproduce. In Newfoundland, Canada, as in Massachusetts, tens of thousands of fishermen lost their livelihoods. The same scenario was played out in Europe. In 2000, the cod fishery in northern Europe was closed to fishermen in an effort to give the fish population time to recover. To date, cod populations do not seem to be recovering on either side of the Atlantic.

A report published in 2003 revealed that only 10 percent of all large fish remain in the world's oceans. The report's author, Ransom Myers, has documented a 90 percent decline in species of tuna, swordfish,

shark, marlin, and other large species such as cod, halibut, and flounder. Catastrophic declines in fish communities are occurring in all seas, from the tropics to Antarctica. Fisheries biologists blame the killing efficiency of industrial fishing practices. This rate of harvesting is simply not sustainable. Fishing pressure is so intense that the majority of fish taken are juveniles that have not had a chance to reproduce.

POLLUTION

For the most part, direct dumping of waste in the ocean by developed countries has stopped. Yet the oceans, particularly along the coasts, are being ravaged by runoff. Every chemical and type of waste on land often ends up flowing into the ocean. In summer, nitrogen-rich wastes cause algae blooms, whose toxins sometimes cause massive fish kills and beach closings.

Sediment runoff from the land is burying coral reefs along our coasts. Research has estimated that at

Bottle collectors find their way along one of Beijing's trash-infested canals. Environmental concerns have taken a backseat to China's economic ambitions. Not only are all of China's freshwater lakes polluted, five of the world's ten worst air-polluted cities are located there.

least 25 percent of commercially valuable fish species spend some critical part of their life cycle on or near coral reefs. Global warming is also destroying reefs, which are extremely sensitive to water temperature. Coral reefs are called the rainforests of the sea because of the abundance of species they harbor. As

reefs around the world sicken and die, so too will the biological diversity of the oceans.

Many fish, particularly large predators, accumulate human-made toxins in their body tissue. DDT, PCBs, dioxins, and similar toxic chemicals are found at dangerously high levels in whales, dolphins, and numerous species of large fish. Today, pregnant women and young children are advised not to eat tuna because of the high levels of mercury it contains.

Oceans are not inexhaustible. Their vastness does not make them invulnerable. Much of today's ocean research is directed at saving our oceans from climate change, pollution, and overfishing before it's too late.

Glossary

barometric pressure The pressure caused by the weight of the air at the earth's surface.

bathyscaphe A submersible vessel with a spherical, pressurized chamber for exploring the depths of the ocean.

continental drift The theory, proposed by Alfred Wegener, that all the continents had once been a single continent but separated and moved away from each other.

crust The topmost layer of the solid earth, including the surface of the land and the floor of the oceans.

current A large body of water that flows in a given direction or pattern.

cyclonic Referring to the counterclockwise flow of air around a region of low pressure that generates storms called cyclones or hurricanes.

echolocation Using sound to locate objects under water.

epicenter The site at which an earthquake occurs, such as where tectonic plates collide or slide past each other.

gyre A circular current in the ocean.

halocline A boundary between ocean currents distinguished by differences in salinity.

magma The melted rock found beneath the crust in the earth's mantle.

mantle The hot region of melted rock beneath the earth's crust.

meteorologist A scientist who studies weather and climate.

monsoon The seasonal torrential rains that occur when clouds that form over a cool ocean move over much warmer land.

overfishing Catching or harvesting so many fish that the fish population cannot sustain itself.

plate A piece of the earth's crust that moves as a result of continental drift.

pressure gradient The difference in air pressure between two locations.

pycnocline A boundary between ocean currents distinguished by differences in water density.

seafloor spreading The ripping apart of the seafloor at rifts in mid-ocean ridges, causing new crust to form from emerging magma.

sonar Echo-sounding; the use of sound waves to determine the type and location of undersea objects.

submersible A craft designed to explore the deep sea with a pressurized cabin and equipment for scientific exploration and analysis.

symbiosis A relationship between two organisms in which both benefit.

thermocline The major boundary, distinguished by differences in temperature, between the ocean's surface currents and the waters of the deep sea.

trade winds The east-to-west-blowing equatorial winds.

trench A deep rift in the ocean floor where the earth's crust (as part of the seafloor) is thrust into the mantle.

upwelling The rising to the ocean's surface of cold, nutrient-rich water from the deep ocean.

For More Information

ORGANIZATIONS

Scripps Institution of Oceanography
8602 La Jolla Shores Drive
La Jolla, CA 92037
(858) 534-3624

Woods Hole Oceanographic Institution
Co-op Building, MS #16
Woods Hole, MA 02543
(508) 548-1400

MUSEUMS

American Museum of Natural History
Central Park West and 79th Street
New York, NY 10024-5192
(212) 769-5000

Monterey Bay Aquarium
886 Cannery Row
Monterey, CA 93940
(831) 648-4800

Smithsonian Institution
P.O. Box 37012
SI Building, Room 153, MRC 010
Washington, DC 20013-7012
(202) 357-2700

South Street Seaport Museum
207 Front Street
New York, NY 10038
(212) 748-8600

Virginia Marine Science Museum
717 General Booth Boulevard
Virginia Beach, VA 23451
(757) 425-FISH (3474)

WEB SITES:

Due to the changing nature of Internet links, the Rosen Publishing Group, Inc., has developed an online list of Web sites related to the subject of this book. This site is updated regularly. Please use this link to access the list:

http://www.rosenlinks.com/gsq/naoc

For Further Reading

Byatt, Andrew. *Blue Planet.* New York: DK
 Publishers, 2002.

Carson, Rachel. *The Sea Around Us.* New York: Oxford
 University Press, 1961.

Crawford, Jean Butte. *Ocean Life.* Alexandria, VA:
 TimeLife Education, 2000.

Doris, Ellen. *Marine Biology* (A Real Kids, Real
 Science Book). Woods Hole, MA: Thames and
 Hudson, 1993.

Knight, Linsay. *Under the Sea.* New York: TimeLife
 Books, 1995.

Pfeffer, Wendy. *Living on the Edge: Deep Ocean.*
 Tarrytown, NY: Benchmark Books, 2002.

Seibert, Patricia. *Discovering El Niño.* Brookfield, CT: Millbrook, 2000.

Trupp, Philip Z. *Sea of Dreamers: Travels with Famous Ocean Explorers.* Golden, CO: Fulcrum Publishers, 1998.

Waters, John Frederick. *Deep-Sea Vents: Living Worlds Without the Sun.* New York: Cobblehill, 1994.

Bibliography

Ellis, Richard. *Deep Atlantic: Life, Death, and Exploration in the Abyss.* New York: The Lyons Press, 1998.

Ellis, Richard. *The Empty Oceans.* Washington, DC: Shearwater Books, 2003.

Fagan, Brian. *Floods, Famines, and Emperors: El Niño and the Fate of Civilizations.* New York: Basic Books, 2000.

Kunzig, Robert. *Mapping the Deep.* New York: W. W. Norton, 2000.

Kunzig, Robert. *The Restless Sea: Exploring the World Beneath the Waves.* New York: W. W. Norton, 1999.

Markle, Sandra. *Pioneering Ocean Depths.* New York: Atheneum, 1995.

Oppenheim, Joanne. *Oceanarium.* New York: Bantam Books, 1995.

Prager, Ellen, J. *The Oceans.* New York: McGraw-Hill, 2000.

Rogers, Daniel. *Waves, Tides, and Currents.* New York: Bookwright Press, 1991.

Index

Credits

ABOUT THE AUTHOR

Natalie Goldstein has been a writer of science and educational materials for fifteen years. She has written extensively about environmental, life, and the physical sciences. Among her books are the *Earth Almanac, Rebuilding Prairies and Forests, Viruses,* and *The Nature of the Atom.* She has worked for the Nature Conservancy, the Hudson River Foundation, the World Wildlife Fund, and the Audubon Society. A member of the National Association of Science Writers and the Society of Environmental Journalists, Ms. Goldstein holds master's degrees in environmental science and education.